RETAIL AND RESTAURANT

ROCKPORT
PUBLISHERS

Rockport Publishers, Inc.
Rockport, Massachusetts

First published in the United States of America by:
Rockport Publishers, Inc.
146 Granite Street
Rockport, Massachusetts 01966-1299
Telephone: (508) 546-9590
Fax: (508) 546-7141

Distributed to the trade by:
Consortium Book Sales & Distribution, Inc.
1045 Westgate Drive
Saint Paul, MN 55114
(612) 221-9035
(800) 283-3572

Other distribution by:
Rockport Publishers, Inc.
Rockport, Massachusetts 01966-1299

ISBN 1-56496-338-1

10 9 8 7 6 5 4 3 2 1

Cover Photographs: *clockwise from top left,*
Bartels & Company, Associates Design,
Associates Design, Penn State University,
Britches of Georgetown

Manufactured in Hong Kong by
Regent Publishing Services Limited

INTRODUCTION

For restaurants and retail establishments, there's no better way to reinforce a company's image than by using printed materials with a strong graphic identity. When a business can show a strong logo in creative and prominent ways on premises, it helps support the name recognition built with advertising, marketing, and word-of-mouth endorsements.

This anthology features the best restaurant and retail graphics Rockport has published throughout the 1990s. Its pages contain signs, menus, interior designs, posters, and table tents that not only show how successful businesses display their image, but also inspire designers to make their own great graphics.

DESIGNERS
Vidette Falmo
Alpha-Graphics
Noel Weber
Kevin Mills

FABRICATORS
Kevin Mills
Todd Hanson
Lana and Noel Weber, Jr.

CLIENT
Dave Boldiga

This 36- by 56-inch sign's letters are cut from PVC. The outside frame is high-density urethane with a copper-laminate inlay. The background is hardboard, painted with acrylic urethane, and the sunburst is gilded high-density urethane, as is the edge of the lettering.

DESIGNER
Lawrin Rosen
ARTeffects, Inc.

FABRICATOR
Brad Butler
ARTeffects, Inc.

CLIENT
Pizzaworks

The sign is layered MDO with painted graphics and dimensional letters.

DESIGNER
Daniel Carlson
Carlson Sign Art

FABRICATOR
Carlson Sign Art

CLIENT
Dan Verhil

This 48- by 54-inch double-faced, redwood sign is completely carved. The oval center is cut through, and the beer stein has been turned on a wood lathe, with the top cut off and remounted. The suds are Great Stuff foam (home insulating material). All the copy is gilded in 23K goldleaf.

DESIGNER
Rick Glawson
Fine Gold Sign Co.

FABRICATOR
Fine Gold Sign Co.

CLIENT
P.T. Copperpott—Universal City Walk

Various techniques are used for each portion of the system including glue-chipping, acid etching and water, and surface and angel gilding in 23K, 18K, and 16K gold, and copper leaf. Other techniques include Japan blending, glazing, and outlining in transparents for painted portions. Included are abalone and glass-jewel insets with a portion of the more than 1000 jewels laminated with dichroic glass.

DESIGNERS
Kraig Yaseen
Al Lowrie
Yaseen Design Studio

FABRICATOR
Yaseen Design Studio

CLIENT
John Kolb
Cammy Kolb

This flat-painted MDO sign is hand-lettered, with airbrushed fades. The illustrations are a combination of hand painting and airbrushing. The copy incorporates vinyl and variegated leaf (below the "S" in "Schluter").

DESIGNER
Ray Guzman
Hoboken Sign

FABRICATORS
Ray Guzman
Renata Guzman

CLIENT
Persis

This sign is hand-painted MDO with a prismatic, drop-shade script. The border is painted to mimic rich texture and textile patterned after Middle Eastern influences. The center oval panel is designed to appear as a three-dimensional logo crest.

DESIGNER
Jack Murray
Jack Murray Design

FABRICATOR
Jack Murray

CLIENT
3rd & Spruce Cafe

The "bottlecap" has an 84-inch diameter and is 18 inches deep. It is made from plywood, chicken wire, barthform, and a spackle mixture. In addition, it has a bulletin-enamel finish and all its elements are hand lettered.

DESIGNER
B.J. Goodman

FABRICATOR
B.J. Goodman

CLIENT
Marv Hall, Tasty Pastry Bakery

The 8-foot by 18-foot by one-half-inch MDO sign is painted with lettering enamels. The sign size is the largest allowed by local sign codes.

DESIGNER
Stan Chavis

FABRICATOR
Roadrunner Signs

CLIENT
Lieber's Luggage

The briefcase is 8 feet by 20 feet, and the luggage tag measures 6 feet by 10 feet. Both use neon, angle iron, sheet metal, and polished aluminum.

DESIGNER
Kris Geerdes

FABRICATOR
Neonistics Custom Neon Studio

CLIENT
Aardvark C.D.s, Tapes and Records

The background on this sign is 4-foot by 4-foot smoked acrylic, and rich blue, white, clear gold, and clear glass tubes create the aardvark image and lettering.

DESIGNER
National Sign Design

FABRICATOR
National Sign Corp.

CLIENT
Coyote Creek Pizza Co.

This is a 3.5-foot by 12-foot extruded-aluminum cabinet with an aluminum cut-edge face. In addition, there is a halo-yellow neon effect behind the face panel. There are also exposed neon skeleton tubes on all painted graphics.

DESIGNER
Jon Ault

FABRICATOR
Jon Ault

CLIENT
Vina Vietnamese Restaurant

This sign measures approximately 6.5 feet by 5 feet. It is mounted on glass frames suspended in a window, with a clear acrylic barrier mounted behind the sign. The neon used includes sun yellow, clear gold, neon blue, and neon ruby.

DESIGNER
Diane Chouinard
Claude Neon Ltd.

FABRICATOR
Claude Neon Ltd.

CLIENT
Café du Boulevard

The coffee cup symbol is fabricated in three separate sections. The square bottom is quarter-inch aluminum. On top are superimposed two reverse steel channels illuminated with white, blue, and gold neon. The letters are reverse channel, illuminated with gold neon.

DESIGNERS
Ray Guzman
Hoboken Sign
Nancy Wykstra (logo)

FABRICATOR
Hoboken Sign

CLIENT
Nancy Wykstra

This sign is reverse-painted with
sign enamels.

DESIGNER
Joshua Winer
Architectural Murals

FABRICATOR
Architectural Murals

CLIENT
The S & S Restaurant

This is a 35-foot by 60-foot exterior wall mural. Keim silicate paint is used directly on a brick wall. The trompe l'oeil painting transforms the blank wall into a historic painted facade. Portraits of five generations of this family-owned restaurant are included.

BY THE BOTTLE
OR
BY THE GLASS

PG

WINE

PEPPERONI

PG

MENU

GRILL

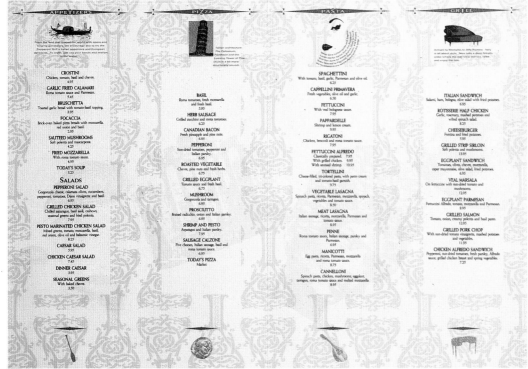

APPETIZERS

CROSTINI
Chicken, tomato, basil and chevre.
4.95

GARLIC FRIED CALAMARI
Roma tomato sauce and Parmesan.
5.45

BRUSCHETTA
Toasted garlic bread with tomato-basil topping.
3.95

FOCACCIA
Brick-oven baked pizza breads with mozzarella,
red onion and basil.
2.95

SAUTEED MUSHROOMS
Soft polenta and mascarpone.
4.25

FRIED MOZZARELLA
With roma tomato sauce.
4.95

TODAY'S SOUP
3.25

SALADS

PEPPERONI SALAD
Gorgonzola cheese, calamata olives, cucumbers,
pepperoni, tomatoes, Dijon vinaigrette and basil.
6.95

GRILLED CHICKEN SALAD
Chilled asparagus, basil aioli, cashews,
seasonal greens and fried polenta.
7.95

PESTO MARINATED CHICKEN SALAD
Mixed greens, tomato, mozzarella, basil,
red onion, olive oil and balsamic vinegar.
8.25

CAESAR SALAD
3.95

CHICKEN CAESAR SALAD
7.45

DINNER CAESAR
3.95

SEASONAL GREENS
With baked chevre.
3.50

PIZZA

BASIL
Roma tomatoes, fresh mozzarella
and fresh basil.
5.95

HERB SAUSAGE
Grilled zucchini and roma tomatoes.
6.25

CANADIAN BACON
Fresh pineapple and pine nuts.
6.95

PEPPERONI
Sun-dried tomatoes, pepperoni and
Italian parsley.
6.95

ROASTED VEGETABLE
Chevre, pine nuts and fresh herbs.
6.75

GRILLED EGGPLANT
Tomato sauce and fresh basil.
6.75

MUSHROOM
Gorgonzola and tarragon.
6.95

PROSCIUTTO
Braised radicchio, onion and Italian parsley.
6.95

SHRIMP AND PESTO
Asparagus and Italian parsley.
7.95

SAUSAGE CALZONE
Five cheeses, Italian sausage, basil and
roma tomato sauce.
6.95

TODAY'S PIZZA
Market

PASTA

SPAGHETTINI
With tomato, basil, garlic, Parmesan and olive oil.
6.25

CAPPELLINI PRIMAVERA
Fresh vegetables, olive oil and garlic.
6.50

FETTUCCINI
With veal bolognese sauce.
7.95

PAPPARDELLE
Shrimp and lemon cream.
9.95

RIGATONI
Chicken, broccoli and roma tomato sauce.
7.95

FETTUCCINI ALFREDO
Classically prepared. 7.95
With grilled chicken. 9.95
With sauteed shrimp. 10.95

TORTELLINI
Cheese-filled, tri-colored pasta, with pesto cream
and tomato-basil garnish.
9.75

VEGETABLE LASAGNA
Spinach pasta, ricotta, Parmesan, mozzarella, spinach,
vegetables and tomato sauce.
8.50

MEAT LASAGNA
Italian sausage, ricotta, mozzarella, Parmesan and
tomato sauce.
8.95

PENNE
Roma tomato sauce, Italian sausage, parsley and
Parmesan.
6.95

MANICOTTI
Egg pasta, ricotta, Parmesan, mozzarella
and roma tomato sauce.
8.75

CANNELLONI
Spinach pasta, chicken, mushrooms, eggplant,
tarragon, roma tomato sauce and melted mozzarella.
8.95

GRILL

ITALIAN SANDWICH
Salami, ham, bologna, olive salad with fried potatoes.
6.95

ROTISSERIE HALF CHICKEN
Garlic, rosemary, mashed potatoes and
wilted spinach salad.
8.25

CHEESEBURGER
Fontina and fried potatoes.
5.95

GRILLED STRIP SIRLOIN
Soft polenta and mushrooms.
13.95

EGGPLANT SANDWICH
Tomatoes, olives, chevre, mozzarella,
caper mayonnaise, olive salad, fried potatoes.
6.95

VEAL MARSALA
On fettuccine with sun-dried tomato and
mushrooms.
12.95

EGGPLANT PARMESAN
Fettuccini Alfredo, tomato, mozzarella and Parmesan.
8.95

GRILLED SALMON
Tomato, onion, creamy polenta and basil pesto.
13.95

GRILLED PORK CHOP
With sun-dried tomato vinaigrette, mashed potatoes
and vegetables.
11.95

CHICKEN ALFREDO SANDWICH
Pepperoni, sun-dried tomatoes, fresh parsley, Alfredo
sauce, grilled chicken breast and spring vegetables.
7.25

RESTAURANT
Pepperoni Grill

DESIGN FIRM
Val Gene Associates

ART DIRECTOR
Lacy Leverett

PRINTING
Heritage Press

The design affords
the restaurant the ability
to print and laminate
menus as needed.

RESTAURANT
Nana Grill

CLIENT
Wyndham Anatole

DESIGN FIRM
Associates Design

ART DIRECTOR
Chuck Polonsky

DESIGNER/ILLUSTRATOR
Jill Arena

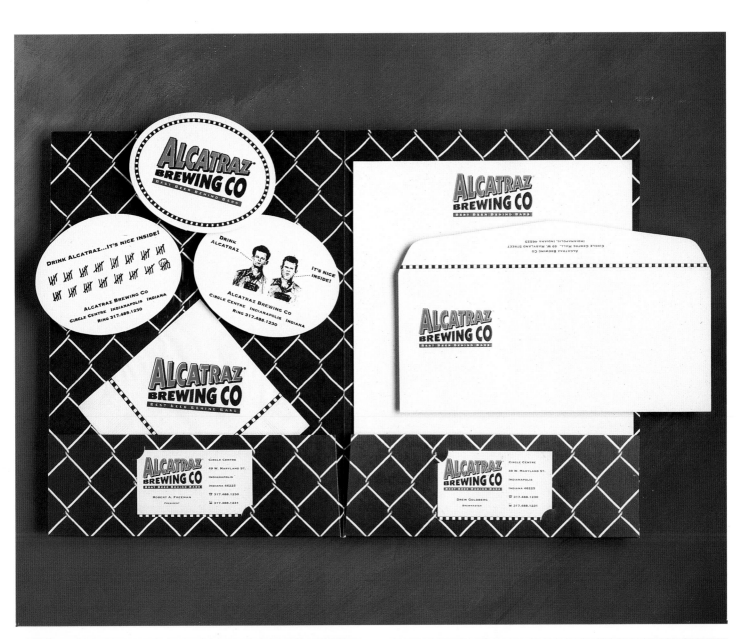

RESTAURANT
Alcatraz Brewing Co.

CLIENT
California Cafe
Restaurant Corp.

DESIGN FIRM
Lance Anderson Design

ALL DESIGN
Lance Anderson

PAPER/PRINTING
Nationwide Sandpiper

RESTAURANT
Longhorn Saloon & Grill

DESIGN FIRM
Core Graphics

DESIGNER
Mike Park, Wes Wickham

The design for this piece was done in Adobe Photoshop; text and assembly in Adobe PageMaker.

RESTAURANT
Rising Star Grill

CLIENT
Metromedia Restaurant Group

DESIGN FIRM
The Beaird Agency

ART DIRECTOR
David Howard

DESIGNER
Laura Trewin

Cedar fencepost used in hill country of Texas, from where the rising star concept comes. When the "TTs" are stapled on, an identifiable character is provided—especially after many have been attached and torn off.

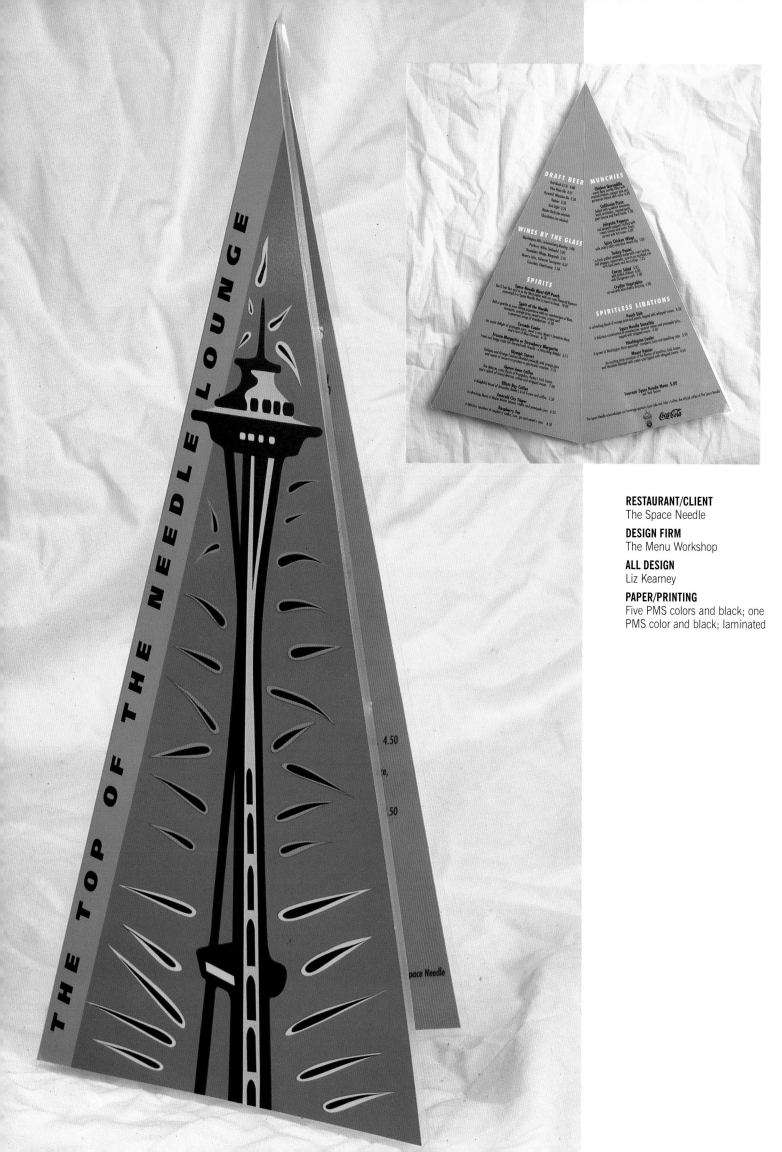

RESTAURANT/CLIENT
The Space Needle

DESIGN FIRM
The Menu Workshop

ALL DESIGN
Liz Kearney

PAPER/PRINTING
Five PMS colors and black; one
PMS color and black; laminated

RESTAURANT
Farah's on the Avenue

CLIENT
Nick Farah

ALL DESIGN
Heather Heflin

Typesetting was done in
QuarkXPress; all illustrations
are acrylic and colored pencil.

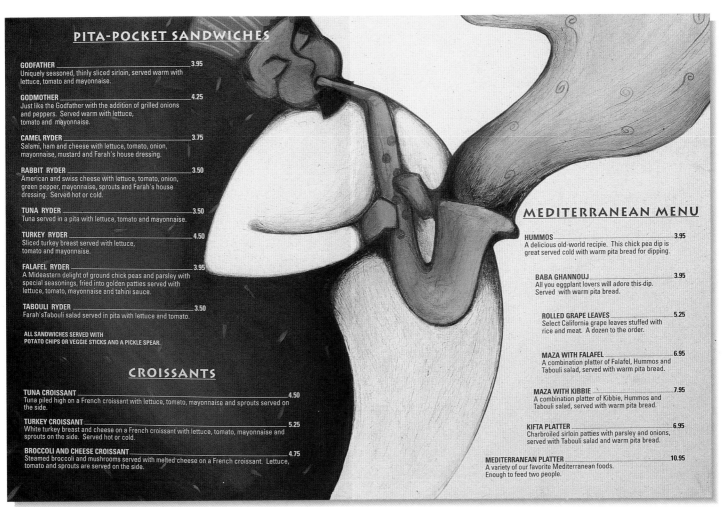

APPETIZERS

BUFFALO WINGS — 10 / 4.25 / 20 / 7.45
The stampede is on for Farah's tasty chicken wings served with bleu cheese dressing and veggie sticks.

THAT ONION THING — 4.65
A fresh whole onion blossom, sliced, hand-battered and fried. Served with Farah's dunking sauce.

CHEESE STICKS — 4.25
Farah's own homemade cheese sticks, fried and served hot with a tomato-ey marinara sauce.

'SHROOMS — 3.95
A basketful of mushrooms, battered and fried golden, served with a dunking sauce—homemade and worth waiting for.

CHICKEN FINGERS — 5.25
Breaded chicken strips fried golden brown and served with BBQ sauce.

SPUDS — 3.25
Potatoes cut the old-fashioned way and deep-fried to your liking.

FRIES — 3.25
A large basket of crispy traditional shoestring french fries.

MEXICALI SPUDS — 3.95
A south-of-the-border flavor of nacho cheese sauce, onions, and jalapeno peppers make these 'taters' a hot item!

SUPER NACHOS — 5.95
A platter of nacho chips piled high with lettuce, tomatoes, onions, jalapeno, cheese sauce, sour cream and your choice of chicken or beef. South-of-the-border salsa served on the side.

CHIPS AND SALSA — 2.25
A large basket of fried tortilla chips served with Farah's homemade salsa.

SALADS

DINNER SALAD — 2.50
A fresh combination of iceberg lettuce, tomatoes, onions, green peppers, sprouts and carrots.

CHEF SALAD — 5.50
A meal in itself, this salad is a mixture of the finest vegetables, cheese, eggs, turkey and ham.

GREEK SALAD — 5.50
Farah's follows the traditional recipie of lettuce topped with Greek olives, pepperoncini, Feta cheese and our house dressing.

SPINACH SALAD — 4.95
A bed of spinach capped with sliced mushrooms, tomatoes, eggs, bacon, sprouts and house dressing.

CHARBROILED CHICKEN SALAD — 5.75
Mixed greens topped with chunks of chicken, broccoli, tomatoes, onions, green peppers, cheese and sprouts.

TABOULI SALAD — 3.25
This healthy salad combines fresh parsley, diced tomatoes, onions, cucumbers, cracked wheat and lemon juice.

SOUPS & QUICHE

Soup of the Day, New England Clam Chowder, or French Onion

CUP — 1.75
BOWL — 2.95

SOUP & SALAD — 3.75

QUICHE WITH SOUP OR SALAD — 4.75
Farah's serves its homemade quiches with a cup of the soup du jour or a tossed salad. Ask your server for daily soup and salad special.

PITA-POCKET SANDWICHES

GODFATHER — 3.95
Uniquely seasoned, thinly sliced sirloin, served warm with lettuce, tomato and mayonnaise.

GODMOTHER — 4.25
Just like the Godfather with the addition of grilled onions and peppers. Served warm with lettuce, tomato and mayonnaise.

CAMEL RYDER — 3.75
Salami, ham and cheese with lettuce, tomato, onion, mayonnaise, mustard and Farah's house dressing.

RABBIT RYDER — 3.50
American and swiss cheese with lettuce, tomato, onion, green pepper, mayonnaise, sprouts and Farah's house dressing. Served hot or cold.

TUNA RYDER — 3.50
Tuna served in a pita with lettuce, tomato and mayonnaise.

TURKEY RYDER — 4.50
Sliced turkey breast served with lettuce, tomato and mayonnaise.

FALAFEL RYDER — 3.95
A Mideastern delight of ground chick peas and parsley with special seasonings, fried into golden patties served with lettuce, tomato, mayonnaise and tahini sauce.

TABOULI RYDER — 3.50
Farah's Tabouli salad served in pita with lettuce and tomato.

ALL SANDWICHES SERVED WITH POTATO CHIPS OR VEGGIE STICKS AND A PICKLE SPEAR.

CROISSANTS

TUNA CROISSANT — 4.50
Tuna piled high on a French croissant with lettuce, tomato, mayonnaise and sprouts served on the side.

TURKEY CROISSANT — 5.25
White turkey breast and cheese on a French croissant with lettuce, tomato, mayonnaise and sprouts on the side. Served hot or cold.

BROCCOLI AND CHEESE CROISSANT — 4.75
Steamed broccoli and mushrooms served with melted cheese on a French croissant. Lettuce, tomato and sprouts are served on the side.

MEDITERRANEAN MENU

HUMMOS — 3.95
A delicious old-world recipie. This chick pea dip is great served cold with warm pita bread for dipping.

BABA GHANNOUJ — 3.95
All you eggplant lovers will adore this dip. Served with warm pita bread.

ROLLED GRAPE LEAVES — 5.25
Select California grape leaves stuffed with rice and meat. A dozen to the order.

MAZA WITH FALAFEL — 6.95
A combination platter of Falafel, Hummos and Tabouli salad, served with warm pita bread.

MAZA WITH KIBBIE — 7.95
A combination platter of Kibbie, Hummos and Tabouli salad, served with warm pita bread.

KIFTA PLATTER — 6.95
Charbroiled sirloin patties with parsley and onions, served with Tabouli salad and warm pita bread.

MEDITERRANEAN PLATTER — 10.95
A variety of our favorite Mediterranean foods. Enough to feed two people.

RESTAURANT
Cup•A•Cino Coffee House

CLIENT
Jennifer Bell

DESIGNER
Gloria Paul

ILLUSTRATORS
Various

PAPER/PRINTING
Wausau Astrobrights
60 lb. text/offset

This project was produced
on a Power Macintosh, using
Macromedia FreeHand.

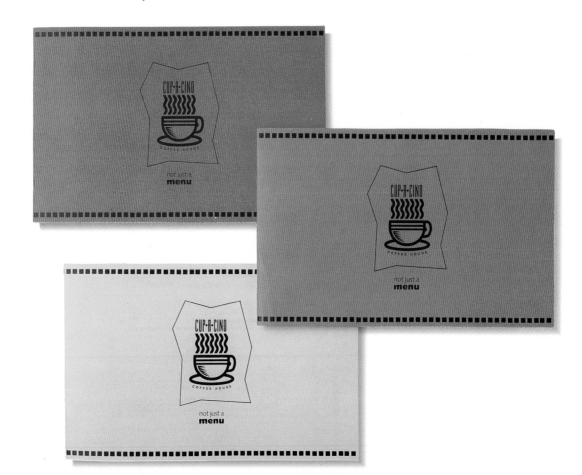

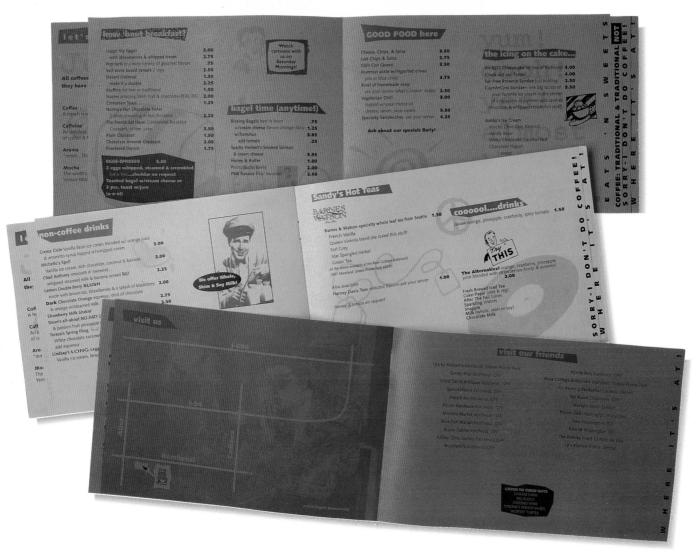

RESTAURANT/CLIENT
South Union Bakery
and Bread Cafe

DESIGN FIRM
Sayles Graphic Design

ALL DESIGN
John Sayles

RESTAURANT
Pulp—A Juice Bar

CLIENT
David Sokolow, Philip Cohen

DESIGN FIRM
Shelley Danysh Studio

ALL DESIGN
Shelley Danysh

This project was created with
Adobe Illustrator.

RESTAURANT
Tony's Town Square Restaurant

CLIENT
Magic Kingdom,
Walt Disney World

DESIGN FIRM
Disney Design Group

ART DIRECTORS
Jeff Morris, Renée Schneider

DESIGNER
Mimi Palladino

ILLUSTRATORS
Don Williams, Peter Emslie,
Michael Mohjer, H.R. Russell,
Jim Story

WRITERS
Greg Ehrbar, Jim Story

PAPER/PRINTING
French Durotone, French
Parchtone (cover silk-screen,
deboss, 4-color process),
Deboss 4-color process,
Warren Lustro Gloss,
4-color process with die cuts

RESTAURANT/CLIENT
Indies

DESIGN FIRM
Jeff Fisher Design

ART DIRECTOR
Todd Pierce

DESIGNER/ILLUSTRATOR
Jeff Fisher

PRINTING
Harbor Graphics

Business card included a blind-embossed palm tree, also used on the menu folder. Identity was created in Macromedia FreeHand; the typeface was specially designed.

RESTAURANT
Fish Company

CLIENTS
Michael Bank, Randy La Ferr

DESIGN FIRM
Rusty Kay & Associates

ART DIRECTOR
Rusty Kay

DESIGNER
Susan Rogers

PHOTOGRAPHER
Bill VanScoy

PRINTING
B & G Printing

RESTAURANT
Wholé Molé

CLIENT
Cornerstone Management

DESIGN FIRM
Associates Design

ART DIRECTOR
Chuck Polonsky

DESIGNER
Mary Greco

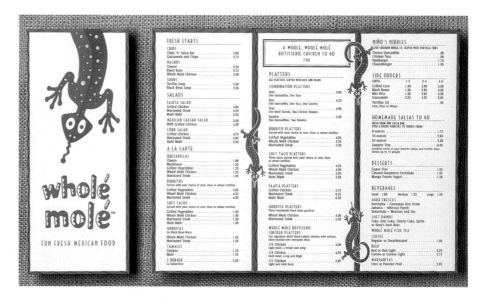

CLIENT
Omni Hotels

DESIGN FIRM
Associates Design

ART DIRECTOR
Chuck Polonsky

DESIGNER/ILLUSTRATOR
Jill Arena

PAPER
French Speckletone

RESTAURANT
Hurry Curry

CLIENT
Michael Bank, Randy La Ferr

DESIGN FIRM
Rusty Kay & Associates

ART DIRECTOR
Rusty Kay

DESIGNER
Randall Momii

PHOTOGRAPHER
Bill VanScoy

THREE WINDOWS
Barneys New York
New York City

**SENIOR VICE PRESIDENT
OF VISUAL MERCHANDISING**
Simon Doonan

VISUAL PRESENTATION DIRECTOR
Steven Johanknecht

PHOTOGRAPHY
The Sandy L. Studio

Mannequin pyrotechnics, simple oriental styling, and randomly arrayed display forms all come under the intriguing and dramatic glow of spot lighting.

TOURING CLASSICS
ZCMI
Salt Lake City, Utah

DESIGNER
Tim Davis

VISUAL MERCHANDISING DIRECTOR
Mike Stephens

PHOTOGRAPHY
Tim Potts

The casual stance of the mannequins helps to portray the casual feeling of Spring '93. Gothic columns are screened on clear mylar on recycled canvas that has been splashed with watercolors and gold leaf.

THE MEN'S WARDROBE SALE
Strawbridge & Clothier
Philadelphia, Pennsylvania

VISUAL MERCHANDISING DIRECTOR
Chris Dixon-Graff

DESIGN TEAM
Maria Boyko and
James Paccioretti

WINDOW TEAM
Julius Jamora and
Marco Angelucci

PHOTOGRAPHY
The Shooters

Suits, shirts and ties fully arranged in boxes attached to the back wall display several possible combinations describing "when to wear it" and "how to wear it."

BENDEL BONNETS
Henri Bendel
New York City

VISUAL MERCHANDISING DIRECTOR
Barbara Putnam

PHOTOGRAPHY
Ari, Sandy L. Studios

Painted faux fixtures and a painted bench create a fun, cartoonish feel to this display featuring spring bonnets. Fresh flowers and pink tissue paper add to the spring feeling.

MOTHER'S DAY
Henri Bendel
New York City

VISUAL MERCHANDISING DIRECTOR
Barbara Putnam

PHOTOGRAPHY
Ari, Sandy L. Studios

Chairs stacked atop mannequin torsos, and laiden with gifts, flowers and accessories, as well as more chairs in the foreground create a multitude of gift ideas for mother.

Photo credit: The Shooters, Philadelphia, Pennsylvania

MEN'S WARDROBE SALE
Strawbridge & Clothier
Philadelphia, Pennsylvania

VISUAL MERCHANDISING DIRECTOR
Chris Dixon-Graff

DESIGNERS
Maria Boyko, James Paccioretti

WINDOW TEAM
Julius Jamora, Marco Angelucci

PHOTOGRAPHY
The Shooters

A sale window doesn't have to look tired. This retailer treated its annual fall event with wit, whimsy, and flying merchandise.

JUNGLEMAN
ZCMI
Salt Lake City, Utah

DESIGNER
Theresa Evans

VISUAL MERCHANDISING DIRECTOR
Mike Stephens

PHOTOGRAPHY
Dennis Potts

This Father's Day promotion features jungle-themed boxer shorts and ties. Brightly colored cloth monkeys were stuffed and wired into position. White rope hung randomly from the ceiling along with large, jungle-leaf GOBO lighting creates a tropical effect.

[ties for money] STYLE A) has letters. STYLE B) has numbers.

DESIGN FIRM
Segura Inc.

DESIGNER
Carlos Segura

ORIGINAL SIZE
6" x 9" (15 cm x 23 cm)

CLIENT
[T-26]

This card promotes a limited-edition silk tie designed by Marc Hauser for [T-26].

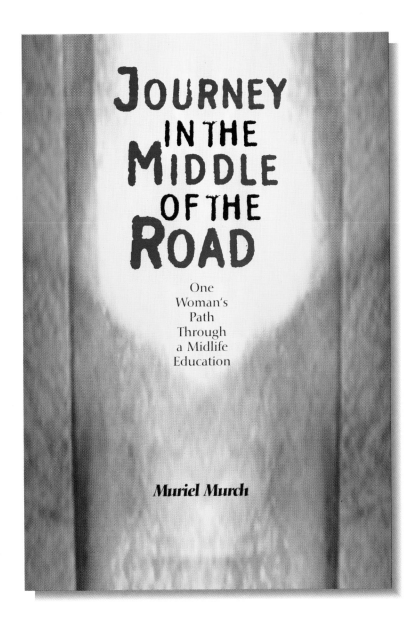

DESIGN FIRM
Design Studio Selby

DESIGNER
Robert Selby

ORIGINAL SIZE
6" x 4" (15 cm x 10 cm)

CLIENT
Sibyl Publications Inc.

PURPOSE/OCCASION
Publicity for new book

PRINTING
Offset lithography

These cards served as mailings and hand-outs for *Journey in the Middle of the Road.* There's space for overprinting late-breaking news on the back side (e.g., "Available at __", "Listed one of top 10 books of 1995").

Ahead of Fashion: Hats of the 20th Century
Philadelphia Museum of Art
August 21st through November 27th

The Shoe Salon on 4

PLATFORM REVIVAL
Frivola Hato Rey
Puerto Rico

ENVIRONMENTAL DESIGN CONSULTANTS
Frank Caballero

DESIGNER
Rio Piedras, Puerto Rico

PHOTOGRAPHY
Mark Bacon

The designers found the comeback of platform shoes very surreal—thus the idea of a three-dimensional painting with a background of clouds and miniature ruins. The tile floor in the frame was placed on a diagonal, displaying the shoes in a "stepping out manner."

PHILADELPHIA MUSEUM OF ART
Strawbridge & Clothier
Philadelphia, Pennsylvania

VISUAL MERCHANDISING DIRECTOR
Chris Dixon-Graff

DESIGNER AND DISPLAY MANAGER
James Paccioretti

DESIGNER
Maria Boyko

PROJECT TEAM
Julius Jamera, Marco Angelucci

PHOTOGRAPHY
The Shooters

To promote shoes on the fourth floor and tip off passersby to the hat exhibition at the Philadelphia art museum, curving wire merchandisers and curlicue frames sport bright fall accessories.

CELEBRATING CHRISTMAS FOR 125 YEARS
Strawbridge & Clothier Philadelphia,
Pennsylvania

**VISUAL MERCHANDISING DIRECTOR
AND DESIGNER**
Chris Dixon-Graff

**DISPLAY MANAGER DESIGNER AND
PROJECT TEAM**
James Paccioretti

PROJECT TEAM
Julius Jamora and
Marco Angelucci

PHOTOGRAPHY
The Shooters

Beginning with a window from 1868
featuring a wooden mannequin,
antiques, and brown-paper packages,
Strawbridge & Clothier celebrates its
125-year history in windows that
span the decades to 1993.
Memorabilia from America's past
appear throughout and include
aluminum gelatin molds and
checkerboard from the fifties, go-go
boots and Warhol prints from the
sixties and a modern-day rendering
of the techno-organic nineties.

DESIGN FIRM
Gackel Anderson Henningsen Inc.

ART DIRECTOR/DESIGNER/ ILLUSTRATOR
Wendy Anderson

ORIGINAL SIZE
8" x 6" (20 cm x 15 cm)

CLIENT
Chocolate Lace

PURPOSE/OCCASION
Summer specials

PRINTING
1-color offset

The designer used Photoshop for the images and QuarkXPress for the layout. The look of summer was created—nice, warm colors to express the time of year. The postcard was successful in bringing people in for the specials.

From the postcard (Summer delights):

Summer delights
from Chocolate Lace

Ah, summer...
porch swings, picnics and warm breezes

Light, refreshing cakes from Chocolate Lace are always a great way to dress up a party table. New this season are Patio & Picnic Brownie Trays, featuring a complete selection of Gail's favorite brownie recipes, and Cool Lime Torte, a light cheesecake with a refreshing lime flavor.

For your summer entertaining, be sure to start your party planning with Chocolate Lace.

NEW! PATIO & PICNIC ASSORTMENT TRAYS
For summer entertaining

A delicious variety of bite-sized gourmet pecan squares and brownies – white and dark chocolate, walnut, cappuccino, turtle and white chocolate. Twenty half-sized pieces on a rattan serving tray. Ready for packing in the picnic basket.

FLAG CAKE
Celebrate Independence Day in a sweet way

Yellow sponge cake topped with fresh blueberries and strawberries. A light and delightful salute to summer.

NEW! COOL LIME TORTE
Sweet Summer Sensation

Tall, light cheesecake, with a butter-cookie crust, cream cheese and marshmallow cream filling, topped with candy lime slices and whipped cream.

BERRY BASKET CAKE
Held over by popular demand

Perfect for special occasions – birthdays, anniversaries or retirements – when a regular cake won't do. A light chocolate sponge cake, filled with cocoa cream, decorated with Swiss chocolate frosting, and topped with strawberries, raspberries, blackberries or blueberries.

COMING IN SEPTEMBER
APPLE BAVARIAN
Zesty treat signals start of fall

A winning combination of creamy cheesecake and strudel with the unbeatable taste of fresh apples.

Enjoy a delicious dessert break at one of our outdoor umbrella tables.

762.0402

Chocolate Lace 53rd & John Deere Rd., Moline
Hours: Tues.-Sat. 10 a.m. to 5 p.m. WE'LL BE OPEN MONDAY, JULY 3RD FROM 12 P.M. TO 5 P.M.

Chocolate Lace
5202 38th Avenue
Moline, Illinois 61265

Enjoy Chocolate Lace gourmet desserts at your next picnic, pool or patio party.

DESIGN FIRM
Belyea Design Alliance

ART DIRECTOR/DESIGNER
Adrianna Jumping Eagle

PHOTOGRAPHER
Roger Schreiber

ORIGINAL SIZE
6" x 4" (15 cm x 10 cm)

CLIENT
The Glass Eye

PRINTING
Offset

The designer created this Christmas-sale postcard in QuarkXPress, importing photos—provided by the client—from Photoshop. The postcard reminds customers to increase the client's Christmas sales.

OG120
Cranberry & White Ribbon

OG123
Blue & White Ribbon

OG110
Ruby with Murrini

THE GLASS EYE ELVES
ARE STILL SHIPPING
IN **10** WORKING DAYS (OR LESS)!

DESIGN FIRM
Art Chantry

ART DIRECTOR/DESIGNER
Art Chantry

ORIGINAL SIZE
4 1/2" x 6"
(11 cm x 15 cm)

CLIENT
Estrus Records

PRINTING
Offset

A general promotional card
for the Estrus record label.

DESIGN FIRM
Art Chantry

ART DIRECTOR/DESIGNER
Art Chantry

ORIGINAL SIZE
5 1/2" x 4" (14 cm x 10 cm)

CLIENT
The Rocket

PRINTING
Offset

The client is a free, monthly
music tabloid in the Seattle
area; the card is part of a
monthly mailing to remind
advertisers that ad deadlines
are approaching,

SEASONS TO REMEMBER
ZCMI
Salt Lake City, Utah

VISUAL MERCHANDISING DIRECTOR
Mike Stephens

PROJECT TEAM
Gertrude Glauser, Anne Cook,
Sherri Orton and Marcelo Zapata

DESIGNER
Mike Stephens

PHOTOGRAPHY
Dennis Potts

Six seasons, beginning with
early spring and ending with
Christmas, filled large store
windows. Shapes were created
with metal framing and
Styrofoam shapes covered
with candy.

HOLIDAY ENCHANTMENT
Jordan Marsh
Boston, Massachusetts

**CORPORATE VISUAL
MERCHANDISING DIRECTOR**
Rita Steffee

VISUAL DIRECTOR
Ellen Davis

DESIGNER
George Arnold

PROJECT TEAM

Joe Clancy, William Glover,
and Catherine Costello

In these windows, key scenes
from *The Princess and the Pea,
Little Red Riding Hood, The
Emperor's New Clothes,
Cinderella, Sleeping Beauty, Alice
in Wonderland,* and of course,
Beauty and the Beast come to
life in modern-day fashions for
men, women and the home.

FLOWERING FIELD'S—A CELEBRATION OF BEAUTY
Marshall Field's
Chicago, Illinois

SENIOR VICE PRESIDENT VISUAL MERCHANDISING AND STORE DESIGN, DESIGNER
Andrew Markopoulos

DIRECTOR OF STORES, VISUAL MERCHANDISING
Jamie Becker

DIRECTOR VISUAL MERCHANDISING STATE STREET STORE
Amy Meadows

PROJECT TEAM
State Street visual staff

PHOTOGRAPHY
Mike McCafrey

This floral event continues the retailer's tradition of an annual celebration as a gift to the public. Flowers fill the store and their fragrance and color fill the air with the signs of spring.

CLIENT/STORE
York Wallcoverings,
Borders & Fabrics

BAG MANUFACTURER
Keenpac North
America Ltd.

DISTRIBUTOR
Commonwealth
Packaging Co.

DESIGN FIRM
Penn State University

ART DIRECTOR
Kristin Breslin Sommese

DESIGNER
Gretchen Leary

ILLUSTRATOR
Gretchen Leary

PHOTOGRAPHER
Dick Ackley

CLIENT/STORE
Red Baron Hobby Shop

DESIGN FIRM
Hallmark Cards Inc.

ART DIRECTOR
Mark Lineback

DESIGNER
Mark Lineback

ILLUSTRATOR
Shoebox Artists

CLIENT/STORE
Shoebox Greetings

BAG MANUFACTURER
Bonita Pioneer

PAPER/PRINTING
Kraft; flexo

Recycled kraft stock, dotted
with featured characters,
reflects the down-to-earth
Shoebox greeting-card line.
Editorial content, brought
into the gussets of the bag,
is a huge part of the playful
Shoebox personality.

DESIGN FIRM
Sayles Graphic Design

ART DIRECTOR
John Sayles

DESIGNER
John Sayles

ILLUSTRATOR
John Sayles

CLIENT/STORE
Schaffer's Bridal Shop

BAG MANUFACTURER
Iowa Retail Packaging

A simple, black-and-white design is elegant and affordable for Schaffer's Bridal Shop in Des Moines. Hat and accessory boxes are also shown, as well as a vinyl gown bag.

DESIGN FIRM
ModernArts Packaging

DESIGNER
Cynthia Di Giacomo

ILLUSTRATOR
Cynthia Di Giacomo

CLIENT/STORE
ABC Carpet & Home

BAG MANUFACTURER
ModernArts production facility, Mexico

PAPER/PRINTING
65 lb. natural kraft paper; flexo

This bag illustrates a unique color combination. Printed on natural kraft paper, it promotes an ecological look.

DESIGN FIRM
Raziya Swan

ART DIRECTOR
Alice Dreuding

DESIGNER
Raziya Swan

ILLUSTRATOR
Raziya Swan

PHOTOGRAPHER
Del Ramers

CLIENT/STORE
Baby Giraffe
African Imports

PAPER/PRINTING
Pantone uncoated

The Adobe Illustrator-
designed logo is applied
to bags by hand, using
cut paper and
Identicolor transfers.

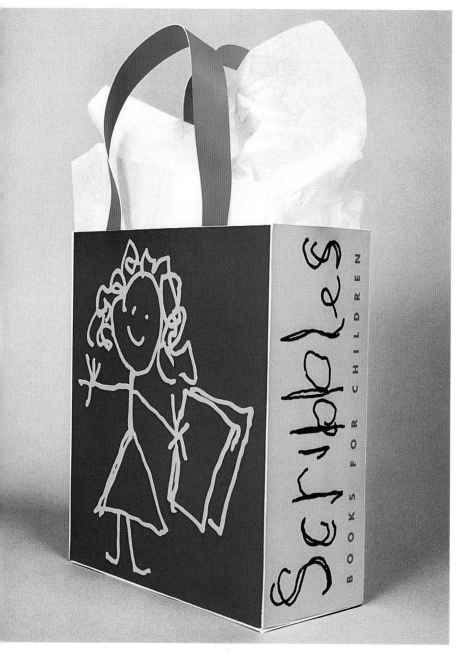

DESIGN FIRM
Raziya Swan

ART DIRECTOR
Alice Dreuding

DESIGNER
Raziya Swan

ILLUSTRATOR
Raziya Swan

PHOTOGRAPHER
Del Ramers

CLIENT/STORE
Scribbles, Books for
Children

PAPER/PRINTING
Pantone uncoated red,
blue, and yellow

After scanning the hand-
drawn stick figure and
the word "Scribbles," the
bag was constructed by
hand, using cut paper
and Identicolor transfers
set in QuarkXPress.

DESIGN FIRM
Howard Decorative
Packaging

ART DIRECTOR
Jen Gadbois,
Lisa Laarman

DESIGNER
Jen Gadbois,
Lisa Laarman

ILLUSTRATOR
Lisa Laarman

CLIENT/STORE
Hear Music

BAG MANUFACTURER
Handelok Bag Co.

PAPER/PRINTING
Recycled natural
kraft; flexo

DESIGN FIRM
Sony Design Center

ART DIRECTOR
Yuka Takeda

DESIGNER
Yuka Takeda

CLIENT/STORE
Sony Style

DISTRIBUTOR
S. Posner Sons Inc.

The Sony Style bags
reflect the clean, clear,
contemporary look of
the new Sony stores,
an updated look from
the previous Sony
Plaza bags.

DESIGN FIRM
Kor Group

ART DIRECTOR
MB Sawyer

DESIGNER
MB Sawyer

CLIENT/STORE
Waterstone's

BAG MANUFACTURER
North American
Packaging Corp.

PAPER/PRINTING
White kraft

DESIGN FIRM
Watkins & Co.,
David Watkins

ART DIRECTOR
Shell Presenza

DESIGNER
Shell Presenza

ILLUSTRATOR
Shell Presenza

CLIENT/STORE
Zales Corp.

BAG MANUFACTURER
Handelok Bag Co.

PAPER/PRINTING
Custom-beaten dyed
black kraft with
calendered top coat;
1-color flexo

Acqua di Giò. A provocation from
GIORGIO ARMANI

DESIGN FIRM
Designer Fragrance

ART DIRECTOR
Miron Swift

CLIENT/STORE
Giorgio Armani/
Acqua di Giò

PAPER/PRINTING
PVC film

DISTRIBUTOR
S. Posner Sons Inc.

This bag was
designed to give the
feeling of water or
lucidity, because of
the lightness of the
product. It must be
shown with the
turquoise tissue
coming out on top
so the imprint on the
bag is visible. The
handle is die-cut so
it will not interfere
with the graphics.

CLIENT/STORE
Muelhens Inc.

BAG MANUFACTURER
PSPCO/12:34
Ltd./Korus

DESIGN FIRM
Desgrippes
Gobé and Associates

ART DIRECTOR
Phyllis Aragaki

DESIGNER
Marion Cledat

ILLUSTRATOR
Marion Cledat

CLIENT/STORE
Victoria's Secret/
Second Skin Satin

BAG MANUFACTURER
Pak 2000

PAPER/PRINTING
Matte-oriented
polypropylene

These miniature
shopping bags were
specially designed
for Victoria's Secret
Second Skin Satin
fragrance, soap,
and bath products.
Because their size
works so well with
the soaps, the bags
almost become the
packaging itself.

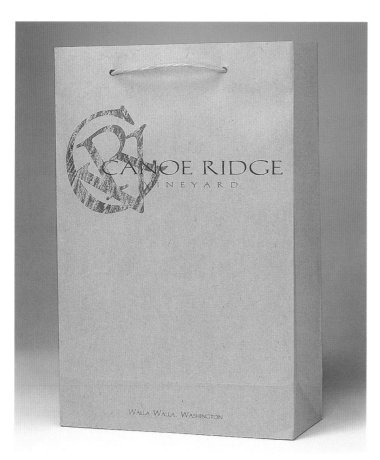

CLIENT/STORE
Canoe Ridge Vineyard

BAG MANUFACTURER
Pacobond Inc.

PAPER/PRINTING
2-color on natural kraft
paper with knotted
twisted paper handles

DESIGN FIRM
Icons

ART DIRECTOR
Glenn Johnson

DESIGNER
Glenn Johnson

ILLUSTRATOR
Glenn Johnson
Client/Store
Vicki Lee Boyajian

BAG MANUFACTURER
Bret Packaging

PAPER/PRINTING
Carnival Groove

The bag works with a
color-coordinated
tissue paper depicting
the client's deco-style
teacup logo.

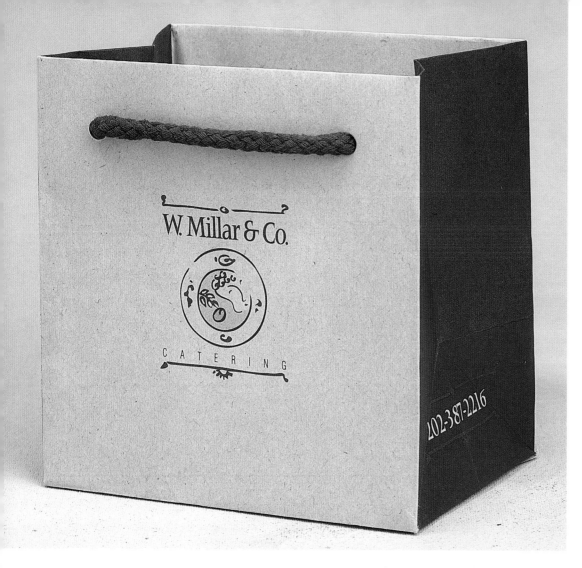

CLIENT/STORE
W. Millar & Co. Catering

BAG MANUFACTURER
Keenpac North
America Ltd.

DISTRIBUTOR
S. Freedman Co.

CLIENT/STORE
The Four Seasons
Restaurant

BAG MANUFACTURER
Keenpac North
America Ltd.

DISTRIBUTOR
Hudson Paper Co.

DESIGN FIRM
Hornall Anderson
Design Works Inc.

ART DIRECTOR
Jack Anderson

DESIGNER
Jack Anderson,
Lisa Cerveny,
Suzanne Haddon

ILLUSTRATOR
Mits Katayama

CLIENT/STORE
Juice Club

BAG MANUFACTURER
Zenith Paper

PAPER/PRINTING
Kraft; flexo

The pastry and take-out
bags were designed in
Macromedia FreeHand.
The main challenge
faced during printing
was keeping the
gradation from filling in
and keeping the colors
pure while using only
four colors that
graduated from deep
red to green.

DESIGN FIRM
Bonita Pioneer

DESIGNER
Jim Parker

CLIENT/STORE
Uniquely Sweet

BAG MANUFACTURER
Bonita Pioneer

PAPER/PRINTING
65 lb. white; flexo

DESIGN FIRM
Penn State University

ART DIRECTOR
Kristin Breslin Sommese

DESIGNER
Nathalie Renard

ILLUSTRATOR
Nathalie Renard

PHOTOGRAPHER
Dick Ackley

CLIENT/STORE
Three Little Pigs
Sandwich Shop

The hand-created illustrations began as line drawings, were colored with pastel, and then duplicated with a color copier. Each piece in the series tells a part of the story of the three little pigs and the big bad wolf. This packaging appeals to the child in all of us.

DESIGN FIRM
Penn State University

ART DIRECTOR
Kristin Breslin
Sommese

DESIGNER
Russel Heim

ILLUSTRATOR
Russel Heim

PHOTOGRAPHER
Dick Ackley

CLIENT/STORE
Rascasse Seafood

Urban-gourmet seafood shop uses bags with a city street scene along with its mascot, "spokesfish" Rascasse.

DESIGN FIRM
Penn State University

ART DIRECTOR
Kristin Breslin
Sommese

DESIGNER
Christine Wilson

ILLUSTRATOR
Christine Wilson

PHOTOGRAPHER
Dick Ackley

CLIENT/STORE
La Boulangerie

Student-designer Christine Wilson originally tried to clean up the illustration and type on the computer, but she felt the design was much better when done by hand. The people and animals in the illustrations are "carried away" by the tempting smell of bakery goods.

NEW OR TOTALLY RENOVATED FULL-LINE DEPARTMENT STORE
FIRST PLACE
Rich's
North Point Mall
Atlanta, GA

DESIGN
HTI/Space Design International
New York City

With roots in Atlanta since 1867, Rich's newest store makes use of pale colors, natural light, and artwork reflecting the current southern United States trend in residential decor.

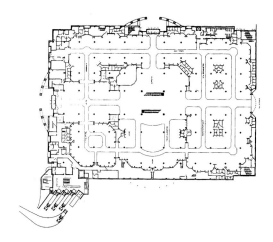

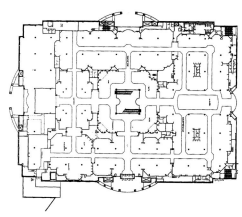

**SPECIALTY DEPARTMENT STORE
FOR APPAREL AND/OR ACCESSORIES
OR HOME FASHIONS AND HOUSEWARES
HONORABLE MENTION**
British Home Stores
Friars Square Shopping Center
Aylesbury, England
DESIGN
Fitzpatrick Design Group, Inc.
New York City

An oval aisle plan paralleled by merchandise walls puts all departments on the aisle with the correct fixture depth in this home furnishings store.

**VENDOR CONCEPT STORE OR
IN-STORE SHOP
HONORABLE MENTION**
Origins
West Broadway, New York City
DESIGN
Peter Forbes & Associates
Boston

Designed with a consciousness
of environmental responsibility,
this Origins features materials
chosen for their durability and
non-obsolescence and a
storefront window set in pleats
to invite passersby to peer in.
Crafted to eliminate the "we
who know and they who don't"
mentality, the shop has no
counters separating staff
from customers.

**SPECIALTY STORE UNDER 5,000
SQUARE FEET FOR APPAREL
AND/OR ACCESSORIES
HONORABLE MENTION**
Wolford Boutique
Madison Avenue, New York City

DESIGN
James D'Auria Associates
P.C. Architects, New York City

To transform an awkwardly long
and narrow space into an
intimate selling environment for
this colorful collection of hosiery
and bodywear, the designers
organized the space into a foyer
with cashwrap, followed by
hosiery and bodywear shops
presenting the line's many colors,
patterns, and textures.

SUPERMARKET, SPECIALTY FOOD, OR CONVENIENCE STORE
FIRST PLACE
New World Coffee
Third Avenue, New York City

DESIGN
Ronnette Riley Architect
New York City

New World Coffee is an attempt to evoke the warmth of experience and aroma associated with authentic espresso beverages. Naturally, earthy, coffee tones, stone, and wood come into play, as do a green-gold backdrop contrasted by cream-colored walls and floor. Lighting and a sharply angled counter punctuated by pendant lights along its edge draw the eye into the store from the streetfront.

**INTERNATIONAL INTERIOR STORE DESIGN
COMPETITION
STORE OF THE YEAR**
Pottery Barn
Chestnut Street,
San Francisco, California

DESIGN
Backen Arrigoni & Ross, Inc.
San Francisco, California

PHOTOGRAPHY
Douglas Dun

Design of this store incorporates an
adaptive reuse of an urban building.
Located on the site of the 1914 Panama
Pacific Exposition, the project's architects
at Backen, Arrigoni & Ross recycled the
antique joists from the vintage 1950
facade to echo the "classicism" of the
Exposition.

The building was gutted and the shell's
wood truss ceiling removed, then put
back with the addition of rough-sawn
cedar plywood. The two-story interior
features a soaring pyramidal skylight
crowning its center. Decorative light
fixtures developed for the store include
pendants and wall sconces.

The walls are composed of the existing
structure's exposed concrete and a warm
taupe Italian plaster. Other natural
materials include Western Red Cedar for
all fixtures, unstained cedar ceilings and a
concrete floor.

The store is divided into three zones:
"Grand Lobby," "Table Top Shop," and
"Design Studio." Decorative accessories
are presented around a fireplace in the
Grand Lobby while all home furnishings
are grouped in the Design Studio in the
rear. Signature displays identifying the
three zones are presented on steel "draw-
bridge shelves" located in niches above.
(This store was featured in the October
1995 issue of VM+SD.)

NEW OR TOTALLY RENOVATED SHOP WITHIN A DEPARTMENT STORE FOR APPAREL AND/OR ACCESSORIES, OR HOME FASHIONS AND HOUSEWARES
FIRST PLACE
Microsoft
Nebraska Furniture Mart,
Omaha, Nebraska

DESIGN
Retail Planning Associates, L.P.
Columbus, Ohio

PHOTOGRAPHY
Jerry Wisler

Designed to encourage curiosity and interactivity, this new shop simplifies software shopping by offering access to Microsoft's full product line and its features. Ceiling-suspended curved graphic panels define department boundaries, while mobilized light wood and stainless steel fixtures allow easy configuration and product mixing. Interactive kiosks are integrated into the merchandising system.

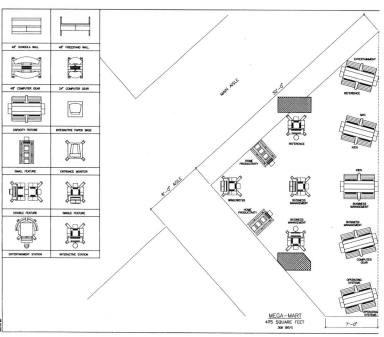

NEW OR TOTALLY RENOVATED SHOP WITHIN A DEPARTMENT STORE FOR APPAREL AND/OR ACCESSORIES, OR HOME FASHIONS AND HOUSEWARES

HONORABLE MENTION
i. c. b.
Bloomingdale's
Third Avenue, New York City

DESIGN
Matsuyama International Corp.
New York City

PHOTOGRAPHY
Paul Warchol

The designers' objective was to create a simple, clear space with minimal characteristics. Fixtures consist of panels—supported by black poles—that "appear to float" between the floor and ceiling. Though simple in design, these flexible units have interchangeable shelves and face-outs. A 360-degree rotating display, located in the shop's center features a graphic panel front backed with shelving. Other merchandisers consist of T-stands and forms with bases inspired by Herman Miller seating. The shop's flooring is artificial stone with steel inlays.

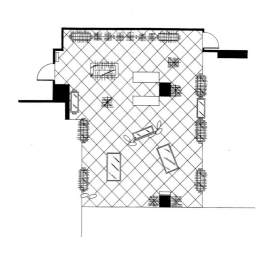

SPECIALTY STORE UNDER 5,000 SQUARE FEET FOR HARD GOODS, HOUSEWARES, ETC. HONORABLE MENTION
Global News
Vancouver International Airport
Richmond, British Colombia, Canada

DESIGN
Sunderland Innerspace Design, Inc.
Vancouver

PHOTOGRAPHY
Rob Melnychuk

This 945-square-foot shop is easily identified by an illuminated, blown-glass globe on its facade. The globe is repeated inside on a curved soffit. An inlaid floor creates a world map as it would appear from space in blues and greens. Inlaid terra-cotta strips represent longitudinal lines that meet at the circular, central fixture. Wall-mounted video monitors provide a sense of movement. Lighting is designed to highlight products during the day and evoke images of stars at night.

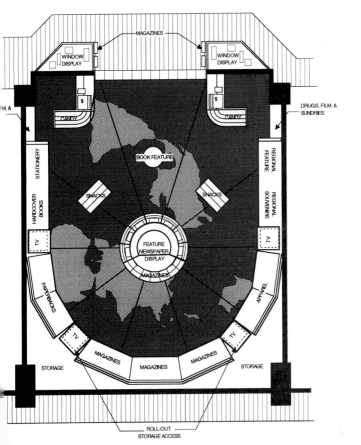

MAGAZINES

WINDOW DISPLAY

WINDOW DISPLAY

CANDY

CANDY

DRUGS, FILM, & SUNDRIES

BOOK FEATURE

STATIONERY

HARDCOVER BOOKS

REGIONAL FEATURE

REGIONAL SOUVENIRS

SNACKS

SNACKS

TV

TV

FEATURE NEWSPAPER DISPLAY

PAPERBACKS

APPAREL

MAGAZINES

TV

TV

MAGAZINES

MAGAZINES

MAGAZINES

STORAGE

STORAGE

ROLL-OUT STORAGE ACCESS

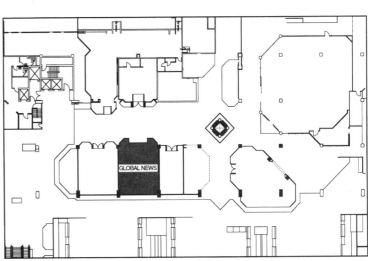

GLOBAL NEWS

71

DESIGN FIRM
Bartels & Company

ART DIRECTOR/DESIGNER
David Bartels

ILLUSTRATOR
Terry Speer

ORIGINAL SIZE
9" x 6" (23 cm x 15 cm)

CLIENT
Sinclairs American Grill

PURPOSE/OCCASION
Restaurant premium

PRINTING
4-color lithography

This fanciful postcard reflects the theme of the Florida restaurant, which gave away the postcard free for the asking. Artist Terry Speer painted the brightly illustrated beach dogs using watercolors.

DESIGN FIRM
Shamlian Advertising

ART DIRECTOR
Fred Shamlian

DESIGNERS
Fred Shamlian, Stephen Bagi

ILLUSTRATOR
Heidi Stevens

PHOTOGRAPHER
Walter Plotnik

ORIGINAL SIZE
5 1/2" x 7 1/2" (14 cm x 19 cm)

CLIENT
Bravo Bistro

PURPOSE/OCCASION
Wave mailing to attract customers

PRINTING
4-color lithography

Bravo Bistro, a casual and stylish restaurant on Philadelphia's "Main Line," attracts a young, professional crowd. Because Bravo's patrons say that the waiters and bartenders are what makes their dining special, they were featured in the campaign. The designer brought the art and photography together with the computer.

DESIGN FIRM
Art Chantry

ART DIRECTOR/DESIGNER
Art Chantry

ORIGINAL SIZE
8" x 4 1/2" (20 cm x 11 cm)

CLIENT
Estrus Records

PRINTING
Offset

A record release promotional for The Mortals' fake spy movie soundtrack called *Bulletproof* comes with a hole drilled in the center of the gun barrel.

DESIGN FIRM
Dynamo

ART DIRECTOR/DESIGNER
Brian Nolan

ORIGINAL SIZE
6" x 4" (15 cm x 10 cm)

CLIENT
Strictly Handbag

A flyer for a nightclub called "Strictly Handbag"—part of a continuing series of various pop-out and-make handbags—gives you something to do while thinking about where to go. Designed in Adobe Illustrator, using Photoshop imagery.

ORANGE ROUGHY

DESIGN FIRM
Sayles Graphic Design

ART DIRECTOR/DESIGNER
John Sayles

ORIGINAL SIZE
5 1/2" x 9" (14 cm x 23 cm)

CLIENT
The Pier

PURPOSE/OCCASION
Promotion

PRINTING
Offset

In this postcard series, designer John Sayles takes a humorous approach to illustrating some of this seafood restaurant's most popular dishes. The designer used special effects such as thermography and foil-stamping on select versions to add emphasis.

RAINBOW TROUT

GOLDFISH

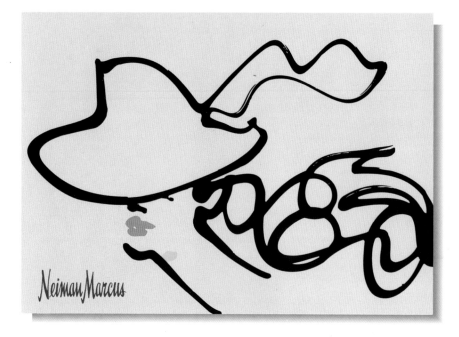

DESIGN FIRM
Rosenworld

ART DIRECTOR
Georgia Christensen

DESIGNER/ILLUSTRATOR
Laurie Rosenwald

ORIGINAL SIZE
6" x 4" (15 cm x 10 cm)

CLIENT
Neiman Marcus

Neiman Marcus created a card for each department of its stores. Shown are the cards for the childrens', housewares, millinery, and holiday departments.

DESIGN FIRM
Britches of Georgetowne

ART DIRECTOR/DESIGNER
Suzanne McCallum

ILLUSTRATOR
Kevin Pope

ORIGINAL SIZE
7 1/2" x 5 1/2" (19 cm x 14 cm)

CLIENT
Britches of Georgetowne

PRINTING
4-color process

Britches of Georgetowne sent this postcard in a direct-mail campaign to reactivate clients who had not shopped at the store for several months.

DESIGN FIRM
Segura Inc.

ART DIRECTOR/DESIGNER
Carlos Segura

ILLUSTRATORS
Tony Klassen, Jon Ritter,
Mark Rattin

ORIGINAL SIZE
9" x 6" (23 cm x 15 cm)

CLIENT
[T-26]

PURPOSE/OCCASION

Promote and generate sales
This card promotes a new
font released by Carlos
Segura called "Time in Hell."

DESIGNER
Sharon DeLaCruz

QUILTER/ARTIST
Sharon DeLaCruz

PHOTOGRAPHER
James Smestad

ORIGINAL SIZE
4" x 5" (10 cm x 13 cm)

PRINTING
Lithography

For weeks, the quilter/artist stood by the
lakefront awaiting the correct weather
factors: a perfect gust of wind and proper
sunlight. Finally, the quilt edges aligned
precisely with the horizon lines. The card
promotes the quilt, which required 2,000
hours of hand-stitching to complete.